The Empty Hand

A Karate Wordbook

The Empty Hand

A Karate Wordbook

by Rui Umezawa

calligraphy by Keiko Tanaka, woodblocks by Sho Hara

Weatherhill
New York & Tokyo

First edition, 1998

Published by Weatherhill, Inc.,
568 Broadway, Suite 705, New York, New York 10012

© Protected by copyright under the terms of the International
Copyright Union; all rights reserved. Except for fair use in
book reviews, no part of this book may be reproduced for any
reason by any means, including any method of photographic
reproduction, without the permission of the publisher.

Printed in the United States

Library of Congress Cataloging-in-Publication Data

Umezawa, Rui.
  The empty hand: a karate wordbook / by Rui Umezawa .
  — 1st ed.
    p.   cm.
  Includes index.
  ISBN 0-8348-0418-2
  1. Karate—terminology.   I. Title.
  GV1114.3.U52   1998
  796.815'3'014—dc21
                                        97-47625
                                        CIP

I would like to thank Kei Tsumura, Shihan and Chief Instructor of Shito-Ryu Itosu-Kai in Canada, for vastly enriching my family's lives through karate; the senior black belts at our school, starting with Hiroshi Maeda and Sandy Sicilia, for their instruction and insights; and my training partner, Alan Janassy, for his friendship and support. This book would not have been possible without the invaluable encouragement and advice from my good friend Meg Taylor, and the guidance of Jeff Hunter, Weatherhill's publisher. I would like to thank Keiko Tanaka for providing the calligraphy, without which this book would not be complete, and Sho Hara for the beautiful woodblock prints. Finally, I would like to thank my family: my parents, for not allowing me to forget my first language; my children, Aria, Kai, and Koji, for all the joy; and my wife Linda, who has to put up with so much because she is married to both a martial artist and a writer.

Contents

Introduction

To Begin ◆ When it comes right down to it, there should not be much talking during karate practice. Most times, you should simply go to class, work up a good sweat, then go home. While you are in class, you should listen carefully to your teacher and do as you are told. This is more or less what it means to study karate.

Nonetheless, there are times when instructions and explanations must be given verbally, and many schools choose to retain the original Japanese terms to refer to things relating to karate. Often, students who have just started karate find the use of Japanese bewildering. This is a shame, because many Japanese karate terms have profound meanings, and being aware of their meaning can greatly increase your understanding of karate, especially if you keep them in mind during practice.

I have therefore chosen a few words commonly used during karate practice that I feel reflect the true spirit of this traditional martial art, and assembled them in this book along with brief essays exploring their meanings. I have tried to go beyond the basic dictionary definition of each term to illustrate how it relates to the philosophical aspects of karate.

This is not a dictionary, so the terms are not listed in alphabetical order. Instead, the opening pages treat words that you are likely to encounter immediately upon starting karate. In the middle I have placed terms to which you will be exposed as you progress in your study, while the closing pages feature terms relating to the spiritual and philosophical aspects of karate.

An index at the back of the book lists other Japanese words that are also commonly used in karate practice but do not possess any special significance beyond their literal meaning. When Japanese words that are featured in this book are mentioned in an essay about another term, they appear in **BOLD LETTERS** to let you know you can find out more about them under their own essay.

A Word About *Kanji* ◆ I also show how each term defined in this book is written with Chinese ideograms, or *kanji,* which the Japanese have also used in their writing system since around the fifth century. Each *kanji* has a separate meaning, and it is interesting to see how these characters are combined to form the words used in karate.

You may already know that some *kanji* reflect the actual physical appearance of what they represent. The *kanji* for *kawa* 川, which means "river" or "stream," is a good example. The three vertical brush strokes depict the flow of water. *Yama* 山, or "mountain" is just as easy to see. The high stroke in the middle with two lower ones on either side clearly depict a stylized mountain peak. Other *kanji* have no physical resemblance to what they represent, and in fact many symbolize abstract, metaphysical concepts.

Chinese characters can be grouped into four basic categories: pictographs, diagrammatic characters, combined-meaning characters, and phonetic characters. Pictographs are abbreviated drawings of objects, as we have seen in the case of *kawa* and *yama*. Diagrammatic characters are symbolic representations of abstract concepts, such as numbers—*ichi* 一 (one), *ni* 二 (two), *san* 三 (three)—or directions—*ue* 上 (above) and *shita* 下 (below).

Combined-meaning characters combine two simple characters to create a new meaning, such as combining "sun" 日 and "moon" 月 to create the word "bright" 明. Phonetic characters also combine two simple characters. One gives the general area of meaning for the new character and the other indicates its pronunciation. For example, the word for plum 梅 is made up of the character for tree 木, which provides the general area of meaning, and another character pronounced *bai* 毎, which indicates the new word's pronunciation.

I have analyzed the characters for each of the words in this book by breaking them into their components to show how they came to mean what they do and be written as they are. The explanations appear on the page with the decorative calligraphy, facing the text for each entry. In my explanations, I have used ancient character forms, because it is often easier to see the "pictures" in them. Sometimes the explanations will provide you a deeper understanding of the meaning of the words; sometimes, they're just fun to know.

Most *kanji* have more than one pronunciation. The ideogram for river, *kawa*, can also be read as *sen*, and the

character for "right" or "proper" 正, for example, is pronounced *sho* in **SHOMEN** and *sei* in **SEIZA**. This is why you may see the same kanji used in two different words in this book, but with completely different pronunciations.

A Word About Karate Styles ◆ If you tell another martial artist that you study karate, you will often be asked: "Which style?"

In contrast to such martial arts as judo, karate is fragmented and divided according to what are commonly called styles or schools. You, for example, may study the "Something-Ryu style" of karate, while your friend studies with the "Something-Else-Kai" school. I hope that whatever style of karate you study, you will respect its history, and appreciate it as the product of much thought and hard work on the part of its founder. However, the existence of varied schools in karate means there are, at times, differences in their approaches to training and the ways in which they execute some techniques. In particular, the list of commonly practiced **KATA,** or forms, can vary greatly from one school to another.

I have tried to keep this book style-neutral. That is to say, as long as you are studying a form of karate that traces its roots to Japan (as opposed to the martial arts of other countries) then most if not all the terms defined in this book should be applicable to your training. For example, I only touch upon two specific *kata*—namely, **PINAN** (or Heian) and **SANCHIN**—which, between them, are practiced by virtually all Japanese schools of karate. I have chosen not to list other *kata*, which are practiced by some schools and not others. You will have to ask your instructor what their names mean.

Despite differences among schools in the practice of karate, however, the spiritual outlook fostered by the martial arts is the same for all styles. I am therefore confident that you will be exposed to all the terms defined in this book at one time or another, just as long as you continue your study of karate.

I hope that by reading this book, what little talking you encounter in karate class will gain greater meaning for you. Best of luck in your training.

Osu!

What is Karate?

This question may be answered quite simply. Karate is a martial art, a form of self-defense. It teaches students to develop fast, powerful punches and kicks as well as skills in joint manipulation and throwing.

You can rightly call it ancient. It was first developed centuries ago on the islands of Okinawa, which is now the southernmost part of Japan. Karate probably originated from the martial arts of China, to which Okinawans were exposed through trade with the Chinese from as early as the fourteenth century.

It is widely accepted today that "karate" means "empty hand" in Japanese. In the 1920s, however, when karate was introduced to mainland Japan, the word was still written using the ideograms *kara* 唐, which referred to China, and *te*, which means "hand." Calling the martial art "Chinese hand" was a recognition of its origins. Later, as karate was further developed in Japan, the first ideogram was changed to "empty" 空, which was also pronounced *kara*. "Empty hand" refers to the ability of karate students to defend themselves without the use of weapons. It also alludes to the influence of **Zen** Buddhism on Japanese martial arts. Emptiness is a central theme of Zen.

Karate's teachings are profound. Because karate can be so devastating, students must always consider ways to avoid conflict in their lives. For the same reason, they must also learn to work together, with respect and courtesy, so that they may practice karate safely and effectively. The ancient traditions of karate also help students to become aware of their places in its history and evolution.

Throughout their study of karate, students are constantly forced to reflect upon themselves, their attitude and their behavior. What does it mean to devote yourself to a goal? At what point are you trying hard enough? Why do you show respect? Why do you follow tradition? When is it proper to use the skills you've learned in karate to defend yourself, and when is it better to turn the other cheek or run? These questions can only be answered through a long, unbiased examination of one's self.

We must also remember that karate often means different things to different people. Young people, for example, often take up karate because they want to learn how to defend themselves. Elderly people, however, may only be looking for an interesting and fun way to stay fit. Parents often enroll their children in karate lessons to teach them discipline and to develop their coordination. Karate is also a very good way to learn much about the culture of Japan.

As you can see, it is quite difficult to completely answer the question, "What is karate?" If you imagine karate as being a deep lake or a pond, then learning how to kick and punch and to defend yourself are only the water's surface. There is much more to learn in the depths below. There, you may even find a reflection of life itself.

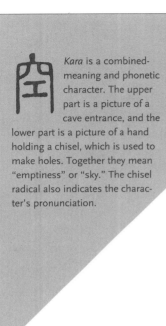 *Kara* is a combined-meaning and phonetic character. The upper part is a picture of a cave entrance, and the lower part is a picture of a hand holding a chisel, which is used to make holes. Together they mean "emptiness" or "sky." The chisel radical also indicates the character's pronunciation.

Te is a pictograph of a hand.

What is Sensei?

In your study of karate, no one will be more important to you than your teacher, your *sensei*. The word is made up of two ideograms, *sen*, which means "ahead" or "precede," and *sei*, which means "life." Put together, they create a new word that means "one who is ahead of you in life." Your *sensei*, your teacher, is your elder and is deserving of respect.

In Japan, teachers are considered to be more than just instructors of a particular subject. They are regarded as role models for their students in all aspects of life. Japanese teachers of math or social studies, for example, are expected not only to know about their subjects but also to lead exemplary personal lives, so that their students may look up to them. This is doubly true for a *sensei* of a martial art such as karate.

You should respect your *sensei* and behave accordingly, listening carefully to his or her instructions and teachings. Your *sensei* is someone who has learned much from many years of intense training. He also has your best interest at heart as you pursue your own studies of karate.

Once there was a famous karate *sensei* in Japan whose training produced national champions. His classes were very demanding, until one day, a thin, sickly boy came and asked to be taught karate. After the boy was accepted into class, the other students saw that their *sensei* was paying more attention to the boy than anyone else. The boy was not very strong, nor was he coordinated, so the *sensei* would often leave one of his other students in charge of the class to take the boy aside for individual instruction.

This was quite frustrating for the other students, especially those who were expected to enter the national competitions and win. Who cared about just one boy, who wasn't very talented anyway, when national championships were at stake? So the top students of the school went to their *sensei* to demand that he devote more attention to them.

To their surprise, their *sensei* said, "You are all very talented karate students. You will no doubt succeed no matter who your instructor is. Therefore, you may leave and study at another school. The boy of whom you speak, on the other hand, is not naturally skilled as you are. He truly needs my abilities as a teacher to guide him properly in training."

When the students recognized their *sensei*'s wisdom and generosity, they bowed their heads and begged his pardon. Afterward, they helped in training the boy, until he eventually grew to become a national champion himself.

Sen is a combined-meaning character. The bottom part represents a human head, seen from above. The top part is a footprint in front of the head. Together they express the meanings "ahead, before, or preceding."

Sei is a pictograph. It depicts a plant sprouting from the earth, giving it the meanings "birth" or "life."

WHAT IS DOJO?

People who practice karate refer to the school or club where they train as a *dojo*. This word can refer to the building that contains the school, or it can refer specifically to the room, gymnasium, or hall where they actually practice. If the class is held outdoors, the field under the open sky is the *dojo*.

Do, the first ideogram in *dojo,* means "the way" or "the path," while *jo* means "place." *Dojo* means "the place where one walks the way." You might think this is contradictory: you cannot, after all, walk very far if you're stuck inside a karate studio. The truth is, however, the time you spend training in a *dojo* can lead you a long way down the path of physical and spiritual growth.

Like other Asians, the Japanese often view life as a journey along a path, beginning at the time we are born and ending when we die. This way of life is a one-way street. We cannot turn around and relive the past. As we live from day to day, year to year, not even one second will ever come back.

In karate, students strive to walk this path the best they can, with honor and with the courage to face any difficulties they might encounter on their journey. And because a moment in the *dojo* when a student is not trying his or her best is a moment of life wasted, karate instructors tell students to perform each technique to the very best of their abilities.

In every journey, we meet people along the way, some of whom will travel on with us. At times when we are fortunate, we develop lifelong friendships through our travels. The same is true of the journey we undertake on the way of karate. The *dojo* is not simply a place to train, but also a place where you will make many friends and gather socially. For instance, it is not at all improper to turn your *dojo* into a party room during the holiday season. At times like these, you and your fellow students may eat, drink, sing, and dance in the *dojo*. The life of a karate student is not all hard work.

Japanese traditions call for paying respect not just to people, but also to places and things. This is especially true for a spiritually significant place such as a *dojo*. This is why you should try and help keep your *dojo* clean and well maintained. You should also bow every time you enter and exit a *dojo*. People often pay similar respect to places of worship. Although karate is not a religion, by paying proper respect we show that we do not take our *dojo*, nor the benefits we gain from it, for granted.

Do is a phonetic character. The left side shows a foot (below) walking down lines representing a road (above). Together they express the meanings "road" or "way." The element to the right indicates the character's pronunciation.

Jo is a phonetic character. The left side is a picture of a mound of earth built to worship the Earth God, from which the meaning "earth" developed. The element on the right indicates the character's pronunciation and also means to purify a religious site. Together they express the meaning "site" or "place."

What is Shomen?

Every **Dojo**, or place of practice, has a side called *shomen*. This side is considered most important by those who practice karate there.

The first ideogram, *sho,* means "proper" or "correct," while *men* means "side" or "face." *Shomen* is a commonly used word meaning "front" or "facade," but it has a special importance in the *dojo*, where it refers to one of the interior walls. The *shomen* can be any side of the training hall or ring except for the one through which people enter and exit.

The *shomen* orients the *dojo* in space. It is a kind of signpost that gives the interior space of the *dojo* meaning. If a *dojo* is a permanent rather than a rented or borrowed structure, the *shomen* is usually adorned with such things as portraits of past karate masters, a work of calligraphy, a miniature altar, or a combination of these. When the chief instructor of the school is called upon to sit formally, he or she will also sit at the *shomen*. Even the ring used in competition matches has a *shomen*, and the main judge will sit toward this direction.

Japanese tradition pays respect to objects and places as well as people. This is especially true of a spiritual place such as a *dojo*. Because the *shomen* is the most important side of the *dojo*, the karate students will bow toward this direction at the start and end of each class or competition match. By doing so, they are expressing their appreciation for their school, its history, and the contributions made by past and present masters. This is no less true when the *dojo* is a rented gymnasium in a school or community center, or even a field of grass when karate is practiced outside. Wherever a karate class is held, there is a *dojo* and a designated *shomen*, and the same etiquette is called for.

To pay such respect is a requirement for all students of karate, regardless of ethnic background or religion. Remember, bowing in karate is an expression of respect, not worship. The small altar that may decorate the *shomen* symbolizes the spirit of the *dojo,* not a supreme deity. You should feel no conflict between expressing your respect toward the *shomen* and maintaining faith in your religion.

Similarly, bowing is not an expression of inferiority, and you should not feel demeaned by being told to adhere to this aspect of Japanese etiquette. In fact, you should observe that when the class bows to the *shomen* before and after class, the instructor does so as well. It would be the height of arrogance to consider yourself above traditions that are followed even by your instructor. Whether or not you are Japanese, regardless of your culture and its history, once you are in the dojo, you should heed the traditions of karate and pay proper respect to the *shomen*.

Sho is a combined-meaning character. The bottom part is a foot, representing walking or travel, and the line on top of the foot comes from the element for country ↑. Originally it meant going to another country and admonishing or attacking it. The meaning developed from there into "to correct," "proper," or "right."

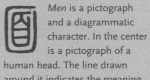

Men is a pictograph and a diagrammatic character. In the center is a pictograph of a human head. The line drawn around it indicates the meaning "face."

What is Gi?

Actually, *gi* is not an independent word in Japanese. It is a suffix or a part of a compound word that means "clothing." When the Japanese refer to the uniform worn during karate class, they call it either karate-*gi* (karate clothing) or *keiko-gi* (practice clothing). Most people who do not speak Japanese, however, refer to it simply as *gi*.

Karate-*gi* are traditionally made of cotton, though it is common nowadays to see *gi* made of polyester. Although today *gi* come in a wide variety of designs and colors, the first ones were simple and white, symbolizing purity. Even if your school does not stipulate white as the color of your *gi*, keep in mind that the appearance of your uniform is, to a great extent, a reflection of your practice of karate. An expertly executed technique can still look sloppy if the *gi* is wrinkled and dirty. In contrast, a clean, bright *gi* can add a vivid crispness to your punches and kicks.

Many schools also display their crest on the *gi*, usually on the left breast, close to the lapel. If your school does this, make it a reminder that your actions in public will always reflect back on your school. If you show poor sportsmanship at a tournament, for example, you will affect people's impression not just of yourself but also of your school. The same is true even when you are wearing street clothes. If people discover you are studying karate, your actions will reflect on karate, so be sure your conduct is always appropriate. Make the crest on your *gi* a reminder of this lesson.

Probably the part of the *gi* that receives the most attention is the belt, the color of which indicates the amount of karate skill and knowledge the student has acquired. Colors range from white to black. The lighter colors, such as yellow and orange, indicate a student who has just started training, while the darker colors, such as blue, purple, or brown, mark the more advanced students. A black belt, as you know, indicates a high level of expertise.

Remember, however, that what is important is not the belt itself but the skill and knowledge it represents. Unfortunately, students often become too distracted by the color of their belt and start to want to attain one rank after another as fast as they can. Keep in mind that attaining belts is not a race. Concentrate more on perfecting your skill, and the belts will come naturally. After all, if it is just the belt that you want, you can always go to a store and buy yourself one.

Keep your *gi* clean. Also, treat it respectfully by folding it properly before putting it away. (If you do not know how to fold your *gi*, ask your instructor.) Take good care of your *gi*, and it will always keep you looking your best as you master those impressive kicks and punches.

Gi is a phonetic character. It developed originally from the character for chopsticks. From there the more abstract meanings of "to take," "to attach" and "to put on" emerged and were assigned to an intermediary character.

Finally the character gi was invented and assigned the more restricted meanings "to put on (wear) clothing" or "clothing." All three characters are pronounced the same in Chinese.

What is Dan?

Many people who are not very familiar with martial arts think that after receiving a black belt there is nothing left to attain in karate. You may, however, have heard those with black belts refer to themselves as a first *dan* or higher. As this indicates, black belts have varying degrees, and attaining your first one is just the beginning.

The ideogram *dan* means level or step. A stairway is called a *kaidan*, or "series of steps," in Japanese. The various *dan* of black belts, therefore, reflect various steps or levels of proficiency after attaining the black belt. Incidentally, *dan* are assigned in a variety of Japanese disciplines, and in most cases these degrees of attainment are not symbolized by different-colored belts or costumes. A Japanese chess expert , for example, will be ranked with a *dan*, though he or she does not wear a traditional uniform.

The number "one" is called *ichi* in Japanese (see the appendix for all the numbers). The first level of the black belt, however, is not called *ichi-dan* but *sho-dan*. This is interesting. The numbers "two" and "three" are *ni* and *san*, respectively, and the second and third levels are, as you would expect, called *ni-dan* and *san-dan*. Why is only the first level different?

In fact, the ideogram *sho* means "first" or "beginning." The same ideogram is used to express the idea of the first sunrise of the year, for example. It is also found in the word for "beginner." The use of the word *shodan*, first or beginning *dan*, for the first stage of the black belt shows that in Japan the student who has only achieved *shodan* is still considered a beginner—a very different awareness than that found in the West, where so much importance is placed on the black belt as a final goal. But once you truly realize the depths of knowledge and skill that can be acquired through karate, you also realize that the few years required to attain your first black belt are really just the beginning.

On the other hand, a wonderful thing about karate is that a limitless number of black belts can be given out. Many things in life, from the number of new job openings at a prestigious company to the number of medals at the Olympics, are limited, and some people will not attain these goals no matter how hard they try. There is no such limit to karate. As long as a student practices diligently, sooner or later, he or she will receive a black belt.

Whether or not you will attain a *dan*, and how much further you develop beyond *sho-dan*, depends entirely on your commitment and effort.

Dan is a phonetic character. The right side shows a hand (below) holding a big stick or branch (above). Together they express the meaning of breaking an object into large pieces, and from that came the idea of steps or stages. The element on the left indicates the character's pronunciation.

What is Senpai?

Karate traditions call upon you to show a great amount of respect to students who have been studying at your school for longer than you have. These students are called your *senpai*. If we think of the relationship between you and your karate teacher, or **Sensei,** as similar to that between a child and a parent, then you should consider your *senpai* to be more like your older siblings.

Your *sensei* is your elder not just in karate but in all aspects of life. As such, you should show your *sensei* the utmost respect. While your *senpai* is also your senior, he or she precedes you only in relation to a particular discipline—in this case, karate. While you must still treat your *senpai* with the appropriate respect and courtesy, this difference makes him or her more approachable.

The first ideogram in *senpai* is the same as that in *sensei*, namely, *sen*, which means "to precede" or "to lead." The second ideogram, *hai* (pronounced *pai* in this case) means "a group of people." A *senpai*, therefore, is a colleague who preceeds you within a group.

A good *senpai* will not hesitate to give you individual help in your training in addition to the instruction you receive from your *sensei*. The *senpai*, who is still a student like yourself, may at times be in a better position to understand your difficulties and frustrations. If you feel you have found a good *senpai*, you should be able to seek that person's assistance in solving any problems you may have in your study of karate.

Depending on the traditions of your particular karate school, there may be times when you are required to recognize a *senpai*'s seniority. When you bow, for example, you may not be allowed to raise your head upright until after the *senpai* has done so, or you may be asked to clean up after practice, while your *senpai* shower and leave ahead of you. In Japan, there are even instances when junior students are required to launder their *senpai*'s uniforms, though you will probably not see anything like that going on in the West.

While you may not look favorably on such obligations, keep in mind that these are opportunities to express your humility as well as your respect for the traditions of the school. Furthermore, the *senpai* are not without their responsibility toward you, either. The relationship between *senpai* and **Kohai,** or juniors, is always reciprocal.

Sen is a combined-meaning character. The bottom part represents a human head, seen from above. The top part is a footprint in front of the head. Together they express the meaning "ahead," "before," or "preceding."

Hai is a phonetic character. The bottom part is a a chariot seen from above, with a car in the center dissected by an axle, the wheels attached to each side. The top means "lined up" and also indicates the character's pronunciation. Together they express the meaning "a group of people."

What is Kohai?

While junior students are required to treat senior students with proper courtesy and respect, senior students are obligated to live up to the respect paid to them. As you continue in your studies of karate, you will see that new students are constantly enrolling in your school. These students, who have studied karate for a shorter time than you, are called your *kohai*, and your responsibilities toward them are considerable.

Kohai is written with the ideograms *ko,* which means "behind" or "following," and *hai (*also pronounced *pai),* which means "a group." A *kohai* is a colleague who follows you within the group.

The traditional relationship between the **Senpai,** the senior members of an organization, and their *kohai* is very much alive in many areas of Japanese society, not just the martial arts. The tennis club at a junior high school, for instance, may stipulate that new members must collect the balls after the *senpai* practice. The *kohai* may not even be allowed to practice themselves until they have put in a period of obligatory service or apprenticeship. When members of an organization live together, such as company dormitories, boarding schools, or training camps for sports teams, the *kohai* will often be assigned menial daily chores, such as cooking, cleaning, and laundry.

While you might conclude that your hardships are over as soon as you have some *kohai* to look after you, the *senpai* also have their own obligation to fulfill for the benefit of the *kohai*. Taking another example from Japan, if a karate team goes out for a meal after a hard practice or a day of competition, the *senpai* are usually responsible for paying for the meal, as well as making sure each of their *kohai* is going home with a full belly. The alumni of the team—also *senpai*—are also often called upon to donate funds to the team and show support at important tournaments, even if this means taking a day off of work.

It may be too much to expect students of karate outside of Japan to undertake such traditional social obligations, but the unchanging and primary duty of the *senpai,* in any country or culture, is to keep his or her *kohai* motivated. You can fulfill this duty by offering individual instruction when the teacher is not available, or by offering words of encouragement to *kohai* experiencing difficulty mastering a particular technique.

The *senpai* must always be vigilant, because the position of power a *senpai* has over his *kohai* can be very easily abused. Hazing, sexual harassment, or other abuses of authority have no place in the *senpai-kohai* relationship or the practice of karate.

Ko is a combined-meaning character. On the left is a picture of a road. The top right is a picture of knotted thread, meaning "connection." Below that is an element depicting a footprint facing backward. Together they express the meaning "following behind," "after," or "later."

Hai is a phonetic character. The bottom part is a a chariot seen from above, with a car in the center dissected by an axle, the wheels attached to each side. The top means "lined up" and also indicates the character's pronunciation. Together they express the meaning "a group of people."

What is Mokuso?

Many people consider karate to be a meditative art, a way to focus and reflect on themselves in the present moment. They want to see themselves as they are now, not as they were yesterday or even a moment ago, nor how they will be tomorrow or in the next second. They do so by getting away from their day-to-day activities—the office, household chores, school, and homework—to spend an hour or two concentrating on getting each karate technique perfect.

If you could make each moment in life a work of perfection, you would be living very well indeed. You would never feel regret that you are not living life to its fullest potential. But this is very difficult if not impossible to accomplish. We all become careless at one time or another, and there are many distractions to keep us from concentrating continually on the here and now. Students of karate try at least to make the time in which they practice perfect. To achieve this goal, they sit quietly, usually kneeling on the floor, for a few moments before and after each class. This is called *mokuso.*

The first ideogram, *moku,* means "silence," and *so* means "to think." *Mokuso,* then, means "silent thoughts." Despite the belief in the West that meditation entails "emptying one's mind," *mokuso* is becoming more aware of one's own thoughts. In fact, the ideogram *so* is made up of components signifying "eye" and "mind." Together, they mean "looking into the heart." *Mokuso,* therefore, is not an absence of thought but a time of mental reflection on life.

During these moments of absolute quiet, karate students focus their thoughts on life at the present moment, on the practice at hand. Whether you've just had argument with a friend, or it's your birthday, or you've just received a promotion at work, you must use *mokuso* to forget about such matters and simply turn your mind toward your training.

The *mokuso* after class is an opportunity to reorient yourself to life outside karate. You may be surprised how you can get a fresh perspective on your daily routine after you've stepped away from it even for a moment or two. The meditative aspects of karate promote a better appreciation of *each* moment in life, inside and outside the **Dojo**.

You can also use the *mokuso* after practice to reflect on the time you have just spent in class. Did you try your best? Did you concentrate the entire time on your practice? As you can well imagine, it is not easy to think only about karate for hours on end, and even your instructor may have thought about something else for a moment or two. The *mokuso* after class, therefore, can also be the time when you pledge to yourself to do better next time.

Moku is a pictograph and phonetic character. The left side shows soot (below) clogging a vent (above), giving it the meaning of "soot" and "darkness." The right side is a dog. When darkness falls, the dogs stop barking and grow quiet, so the character expresses the meaning of "silence" and "stillness."

So is a combined-meaning character. The radical on the lower right is a picture of a heart. Above that is a picture of an eye. Together they express the meaning "to look into the heart," or "to think, to reflect." The radical on the left indicates pronunciation.

What is Seiza?

Sitting properly on the floor is a vital part of many Japanese disciplines, from flower arranging and the tea ceremony to karate. People who have studied traditional Japanese art forms are very familiar with the way of sitting called *seiza,* which can be extremely uncomfortable to Westerners who are accustomed to sitting on chairs.

Seiza is made up of the ideogram *sei,* which means "proper," and *za,* which means "seat." Maintaining a straight and unwavering posture is one of the basics of proper etiquette in both Japan and the West.

To sit in the *seiza* fashion, kneel on the floor with your insteps flat and sit back on your heels. Women should keep their knees together, while gentlemen should keep theirs about a fist or two apart. Your back should be straight, and your hands should rest lightly on your lap. (How one's hands are placed in *seiza* can differ according to the school.) The chin is pulled in slightly, the back is straight, and the right instep should be crossed over the left sole. And, most important, one should be relaxed.

Japanese of the older generation, who grew up sitting on the floor, are accustomed to *seiza* and they do not find it as uncomfortable as most Westerners do. (Most younger Japanese have just as much trouble as Westerners do.) Many elderly Japanese, on the other hand, will tell you that they find sitting in *seiza* to be more comfortable and relaxing than sitting on a chair.

But if seiza is supposed to be *comfortable,* why so much attention to detail?

Traditionally, *seiza* occupies a position similar to the "at ease" stance in the Western military. You are not at strict attention, but are not completely relaxed either. Of course, during karate practice, students are never *completely* relaxed. Even in between exercises and drills, you must remain focused on karate. If the instructor is giving direction or is demonstrating a technique, you must pay careful attention. And a true martial artist also always keeps at least a small portion of his or her mind wary of unexpected attacks.

By paying detailed attention even to the way in which you sit, you are ensuring that your mind will remain alert and focused, even at times in class when you are allowed to relax a bit. This is why, according to tradition, you should be sitting in *seiza* during **Mokuso** (meditation), listening to your instructor lecture on various aspects of karate, or watching a sparring match or demonstration. You should never sit sloppily or lean against a wall.

Sitting *seiza* is yet another way to ensure that not one moment during karate class is wasted or spent idle.

 *Sei* (pronounced *sho* in *shomen*) is a combined-meaning character. The bottom part is a foot, representing walking or travel, and the line on top of the foot comes from the element for country ↑. Originally it meant going to another country and admonishing or attacking it. The meaning developed into "to correct," "proper," or "right."

Za is a combined-meaning and phonetic character. The top element is a picture of a roof, meaning a dwelling. Inside it is the character for "to sit." It consists of two people sitting on the earth. Together, the character means the place where people sit inside a dwelling, or "a seat."

What is Kihon?

*K*ihon, which means "basics" or "rudiments," is made up of two characters. *Ki* means "foundation" or "root." At the bottom of the ideogram is the radical *tsuchi*, which means "earth." *Hon* means "base" or "at the foot of." It is made up of the ideogram for "tree" with a dash at its bottom indicating its base. The two characters repeat a single, basic idea. This redundancy is an indication of the importance Japanese place on mastering the basic knowledge and skills of a discipline.

Japanese educators have traditionally believed that only by thoroughly mastering the basics can a student develop the skills and knowledge necessary to move on to more sophisticated, creative levels of a discipline. It is therefore not surprising that a traditional Japanese martial art such as karate also stresses the importance of basics.

Like the two characters that make up *kihon,* basics in karate also work from the ground up. The foundation of all karate techniques lies in the way in which one stands. Karate stances are designed to teach students to fully utilize the lower torso in both training and actual combat. The difficult stances strengthen the legs and hips, and by mastering them you can generate more power in your kicks and punches.

In fact, not so long ago a beginning student of karate would not be allowed to practice anything but a handful of stances. All karate stances can be painfully tiring when held over a prolonged period of time, and the student had to learn to endure this pain and exhaustion before going on to further study. This period sometimes lasted weeks, even months, after which the student was finally taught to . . . walk. After that, the student devoted an equally long period to just walking back and forth.

Only after mastering standing and walking was a student taught to block, punch, and kick. As you can imagine, this curriculum tested the student's patience to the extreme. Instructors felt this developed character and at the same time weeded out those lacking the mettle to succeed in karate.

In recent in years, especially in the West, there has been less emphasis placed on basics. Certainly it would be difficult for a proprietor of a karate school in today's fast-paced society to attract or retain new students if all they were taught for the first few months were standing and walking. However, just as a building cannot stand without the proper foundation, and as a tree falls over without its roots, advanced karate techniques cannot be mastered without mastering these basics first.

As you are taught a variety of techniques, therefore, you should constantly keep up your practice of your stances and footwork—your *kihon,* or base.

Ki is a phonetic character. The bottom means "earth." The top indicates pronunciation and also means "beginning." The beginning of any earthwork is its foundation.

Hon is a pictograph and a digrammatic character. It represents a tree, with the branches going up and the roots going down. The mark across the roots indicates the meaning of "root" or "base."

What is Tsuki (zuki)?

Tsuki means "thrust," "jab," or, especially in karate, "punch." When combined with another word, *tsuki* is often pronounced *zuki*, as in *gyaku-zuki*, or "reverse punch." A drawing of a closed fist is used as a logo by many karate schools. The simple punch is the most fundamental mode of attack in karate. It is the staple of karate practice.

There is a saying in karate, "One strike, certain kill." In fact, a large part of training is conditioning your hands so that they are able to deliver blows powerful enough to render an opponent unconscious, and also to withstand the shock of such a strike's impact on your hands. This is done by doing push-ups on closed fists, and by striking a heavy bag or a *makiwara,* a vertical post wrapped in rope. (In conditioning your hands, however, be aware of safeguards against damages repeated stress can inflict on your bones and joints.)

The true meaning of the saying, however, is far more than simply gaining the ability to harm others. It reflects the truth that in life there are often no second chances. In self-defense, this is true in the most practical and immediate sense. If you do not make use of every opportunity to defeat an attacker, the consequences may be dire. But the same truth holds in other, more common aspects of life. Most people have experienced missed opportunities: shying away from a job promotion because it involved travel to an unfamiliar country; not expressing romantic feelings toward another, and never knowing if they may have been mutual; a moment's distraction in a race resulting in defeat; a lack of preparation resulting in a failed examination.

These examples illustrate the importance of staying alert for all opportunities that come your way, and being prepared to fully exploit them.

Thus, when you practice your punches in karate—and you will practice them countless times—strive to make each one as powerful as you can. Deliver each with spirit, as though you are really defending yourself and each strike has to "kill." Devote your full attention to proper technique, maximizing the opportunities with which your imaginary opponents present you.

And as you do this repeatedly in your karate training, you will find that you are growing better able to maximize the opportunities with which life presents you as well.

Tsuki is a combined-meaning character. The top is a picture of the opening of a cave. At the bottom is a dog rushing out of the cave. Together they mean a sudden thrust or attack.

The second character is the Japanese syllable *ki*, adding a noun ending to the word.

What is Keri (geri)?

Without a doubt, the most flamboyant karate techniques are its kicks. Amazing acrobatic kicks are mainstays of martial arts movies. The Japanese word for "kick" is *keri*, and its ideogram is made up of the radicals "foot" and "fast." The word's pronunciation can change to *geri* when combined with other words to form compounds. "Front kick," for example, is *mae-geri*.

When children start karate, they are often most eager to learn the kicks. Unfortunately, the kicking techniques are among the more difficult to master, and the beautiful high kicks demonstrated over and over again in the movies are usually not very practical in real self-defense. The distance the foot has to travel from the ground to the opponent's head provides your opponent many opportunities to counterattack, and extending the foot so high also seriously compromises your balance and maneuverability. The most effective kicks, therefore, tend to target the lower body. The knees and the groin are very good targets for stopping attackers with one strike.

Does this mean students of karate should only practice kicking to the lower body? Not quite. An effective kick, regardless of height, requires power, strength, and balance, all of which can be better developed by practicing high kicks. Instructors will tell you that it is always good to be able to kick higher than you need to.

You may have had the experience of giving a speech or performing a piece of music in front of an audience. If you have, you know that practicing just enough to get through your piece once or twice without a mistake is not enough to guarantee a good performance. Although it is true that the audience will hear your speech or musical performance only once, you must practice until you are able to perform it ten, twenty, or even fifty times without a mistake. This is because when we are in front of audience, we are often nervous, and cannot perform as well as we do in practice. If you have only mastered your task sufficiently to complete it perfectly once, it's very unlikely that your one success will occur in front of an audience.

The same is true in self-defense, when you will probably be even more nervous than when performing in front of an audience. If you can barely kick to an opponent's knees during practice, there's a good possibility you will not be able to do so effectively in a real situation of danger. Only by practicing high kicks can you be confident of defending yourself with low kicks.

In karate, as in life, the best way to increase your chances of attaining a particular goal is by aiming higher.

Keri is a phonetic character. The left side means "leg," and the right side means "fast" and also indicates pronunciation. Together they mean "to kick" or "kick."

The second character is the Japanese syllable *ri*, adding a noun ending to the word.

What is Kiai?

Anyone who has ever seen a karate demonstration knows that karate masters always shout when they punch or kick. And they shout very loudly. You might even say they scream. This is called *kiai*.

Many Asians believe that there is a force that flows through all things, making them move and change. This is called *ki* in Japanese (*chi* or *qi* in Chinese). The weather, for example, which is always changing, is called *tenki,* or "heavenly *ki.*"

People have *ki* as well, although most times we are not even aware of it. You may, however, have had the experience of being tired one minute and full of energy the next, just because something—a sudden invitation to a party, or a impending deadline for a term paper—stimulated you. And when people are very scared or very angry or excited, they sometimes find that they are stronger than they've ever been. Some Asians explain this by saying that in these situations, people are intuitively focusing their *ki* in just the right way to give themselves incredible energy. Some martial artists believe that with practice, you can learn to control your *ki* to give yourself this energy whenever you want. A part of this is the screaming, the *kiai,* which means "working with *ki*" or "harmonizing *ki*."

But you don't have to believe in *ki* to understand why shouting might make your karate techniques stronger. By shouting, you are making sure you are exhaling at the time of attack, which in turn ensures that you are relaxed, and experts in all sports say that you are your strongest and fastest when you are relaxed. This is why bodybuilders exhale when they are lifting weights, and why you can hear, even on television, the sharp exhalation of boxers whenever they punch. This also is why all karate instructors, whether or not they believe in *ki*, believe that *kiai* is very important.

A proper *kiai* comes not from the lungs but from the lower abdomen, or **Tanden**. Ask your instructor for guidance in proper breathing, which should include directions on how to *kiai* effectively. Do not repeatedly shout from your lungs as this can tire you very quickly and even damage your throat.

As you continue your study, you may become more motivated in class whenever you and your classmates make loud *kiai* during your drills. A good *kiai* can also motivate you to retaliate when you are on the receiving end of a particularly daunting attack. When you become more aware of your breathing in general, you should also see an increase in your stamina and strength.

And, of course, when you are actually defending yourself, a sudden, loud scream may scare away an attacker before you have to strike even a single blow.

Ki is a phonetic character. The top part is a picture of steam. Beneath and inside it is an abbreviated picture of a rice stalk, which indicates pronunciation. Together rice and steam came to have the meaning "energy."

Ai is a combined meaning character. The lower part is the mouth of a pot, and the upper part is its lid. Together they have the meaning of "matching."

What is Tanden?

anden refers to the human body's center of gravity, which is the lower abdominal area below the navel. According to traditional Asian beliefs, this is also the area from which the body relays a form of energy that is called *ki* in Japanese, the energy that moves and changes all things in the universe (see **Kiai**). *Ki* and *tanden* are essential elements in all forms of traditional East Asian medicine, from acupuncture and shiatsu to herbal medicine.

Tan refers to the essence of Asian medicine, and *den* means "rice field." The *tanden* is not a single point but a field spread out across the lower abdomen which, like a rice paddy, can be divided into sections. The ideogram is a view of a rice paddy from above. People who actively develop their *ki,* whether doctors of Asian medicine or martial artists, often refer to various sections of the *tanden.*

A detailed description of the theories behind traditional Asian medicine is not within the scope of this book. It should be noted, however, that even if you are not a believer in *ki,* you should still be aware that any activity in karate, from breathing to spinning kicks, should originate in the *tanden.*

A simple straight punch, for example, would not be very effective if you only moved your arm and shoulders. When you launch a straight punch toward an opponent in front of you, you should step forward and lower your weight onto your front knee and fully extend your back leg for the greatest power. In other words, you should make certain that your *tanden* moves in coordination with your fist, arm, and shoulder. Even if you are punching from a stationary position, you must turn your hips as you extend the arm, essentially twisting your upper body around the *tanden,* or the strike will have very little force behind it. Like everything in karate, the greatest power comes from the lower body, where the *tanden* is located.

Similarly, when you breathe, you should use your lower diaphragm rather than your chest and shoulders. Using your upper body to breathe tends to tense your shoulders, which hinders movement. By focusing your breathing toward your *tanden,* your breaths will be deeper and your more body relaxed and limber.

You don't need to believe in *ki* to apply your *tanden* in practice. In fact, the existence of *ki* and its effectiveness in combat is the subject of much discussion in martial arts circles. Some are believers; others are not. Most martial artists, however, will agree that regardless of their opinion of *ki,* an awareness of one's center of gravity, the *tanden,* is essential in developing proper technique.

Tan is a pictograph and diagrammatic character. The dot in the middle represents cinnabar, a mineral to which the Chinese ascribed magical, life-giving properties. The box around it is a picture of the hole from which cinnabar is extracted.

Den is a pictograph of a rice paddy seen from above, crisscrossed by the raised earthen pathways between the paddies. It means "field."

What is Kumite?

Kumite means training with a partner. It is made up of the characters *kumi*, which means "to cross," and *te*, or hand. *Kumite* therefore means "crossing hands" with the person with whom you are working.

There are two kinds of *kumite*. The first, called *yakusoku kumite*, or "agreement kumite," is a form of practice in which both partners agree upon a particular attack and a counter, and practice these techniques repeatedly. For example, the agreement may be that one partner attack with a punch, which the other blocks and counters with a kick. The two then practice this sequence over and over. In this kind of training, each partner can focus on perfecting specific techniques without fear of the other reacting in unpredictable ways.

When practicing *yakusoku kumite,* you should focus on timing and proper technique. A cooperative partner provides the perfect opportunity for you to concentrate on polishing your form.

The other kind of kumite is called *jiyu kumite,* or "free *kumite.*" The partners fight each other freely, using any techniques at their disposal that are within limits of safety. This training sharpens your reflexes and teaches you to look for openings in your opponent's defenses, as well as to predict when and how your opponent will attack you.

The way in which *jiyu kumite* is conducted differs according to school, but there is always a great deal of consideration given to safety. After all, it is rather pointless studying karate to defend yourself if you are constantly getting hurt in karate class.

Nonetheless, there is no question that karate training involves some risk of injury. Just as you cannot learn to swim without getting wet, you cannot learn to defend yourself without acquiring a few bruises along the way. But there is a way to ensure that your *kumite* training is as safe as possible, and it is, once again, cooperation. Keep in mind that even during *jiyu kumite,* you are working *with* your partner so that both of you can improve your skills. A bit of competitive spirit is fine, but harming your partner is not the objective of *jiyu kumite.* Presumably, you want to continue your practice, and you will not be able to if you constantly injure your training partners.

Treat your partner with respect, and concern yourself with his or her safety, and the same consideration will be given to you.

Kumi is a combined-meaning and phonetic character. The element on the left is a picture of the lumpy raw silk thread spun from a silk cocoon. The element on the right is a set of stacked boxes, which also indicates the character's pronunciation. Together these elements express the meaning of interwoven threads, "to cross" or "to join."

Te is a pictograph of a hand.

What is Ippon?

In Japanese martial arts competition, a full point scored during free sparring matches is called *ippon*. Though *ippon* simply means "one point," in karate this score is given to a technique that in real combat would have been a debilitating or killing blow. The same conventions are followed in other Japanese martial arts such as judo and kendo. Although modern matches can go up to three points, a great deal of weight is placed upon each point because, had the conflict been real, the person scored against could have forfeited his or her life. Each *ippon* is a very serious warning and lesson.

For this reason, it was traditionally considered bad practice to hold back against opponents who seemed they could be defeated easily. Things can happen very fast in sparring matches, and even the most inept competitor will score a point from time to time. The *ippon* scoring system served to remind competitors who held back because they underestimated their opponents that the consequence of such arrogance could have been, under different circumstances, much more dire.

Today, when judo is an Olympic sport and amateur and professional karate competitions draw large audiences, more and more martial artists regard sparring matches as sport rather than as a simulation of real combat. This has given rise to such strategies as sacrificing power for speed in non-contact matches, or adopting evasive tactics when ahead in points (though of course there is no such thing as waiting out a round in a real fight). The more dangerous techniques, the ones which are the most effective in real situations, have also, understandably, been made illegal in sport sparring.

That karate competition is gaining such wide appeal is no doubt a positive trend, and, when you are given a set of parameters in which to compete, you should use every acceptable strategy to win, even if it is not always realistic. As a martial artist, however, you should remember that the parameters of sport are different from those of real combat, and that ultimately karate is preparing you for the latter. Competition is an opportunity to test your techniques and your mettle in a controlled and relatively safe environment.

In other words, while it is all very fine to focus on competition, you should not forget the core meaning of *ippon*: a dangerous or fatal blow.

Ichi, here read *i*, is a diagramatic character for "one."

Pon, (also pronounced *hon*) is a pictograph and a diagrammatic character. It is a picture of a tree with a line drawn across the root, indicating a meeting of "root" or "base." It is also used as a word to count some things, which is how it is used here: "one strike."

What is Waza-ari?

Japanese martial arts matches are measured in points called **Ippon**. *Ippon* means that the technique which scored the point would incapacitate an opponent in a real situation. (This is true of each full point scored in a match, even if you need to score three points to win.) Recognizing that there are techniques that may not result in victory by themselves but nonetheless can contribute toward it, half points, called *waza-ari*, are also recognized in competition.

Although rules of competition in karate vary greatly according to the style, a strike such as a controlled reverse punch to a vital spot like the back of the head may constitute an *ippon*. On the other hand, a quick jab that simply catches your opponent off guard may be considered a *waza-ari*, because effective as it may be it would not by itself be enough to defeat your opponent in a real situation. Usually, two *waza-ari* constitute an *ippon*.

The term stresses the importance of technique in karate matches, as the first ideogram, *waza*, means "technique" or "skill," while *ari* means "to be present" or "exists." In other words, in a martial arts competition, physical attributes such as size and strength are less valued than techniques. *Waza-ari* is a term that affirms that technique, not luck or brute force, scored the half-point.

Ideally, points in karate matches should be awarded only to techniques of merit. You might succeed in hitting someone, for example, by flailing away blindly with your hands, but this is hardly karate. When you compete, you should strive to maintain a level of discipline in your techniques worthy of the term "martial art."

In reality, however, even sloppy techniques are awarded *waza-ari* or, at times, even *ippon*. In addition to practical considerations, such as the impossibility of objectively defining what is and is not proper technique, you should remember that in real combat, even a blindly thrown punch can cause you injury, and you will not have the option of complaining to a referee. Thus, even when techniques are sloppy, as long as they are within the rules, *waza-ari* are awarded because competitors should not allow such strikes to slip by their defenses.

Quite often in karate, you are called upon to maintain a higher level of discipline for yourself than you demand of others, and this is such a situation: in competition, always be certain that your techniques meet proper standards, while understanding that scores will be awarded to your opponent even if his or her techniques do not rise to the level by which you measure yourself.

 *Waza* is a combined-meaning and phonetic character. The element on the left is a picture of a hand. The right side shows another hand holding a branch. Together they express the meaning of using a branch as a tool to perform a task, giving the character the meaning of "skill" or "technique."

 *Ari*, a noun form of the verb *aru*, "to be or exist," is a combined-meaning phonetic character. It shows a hand (right) offering a piece of meat (left), and expressed the meaning of "offering," then "holding," and finally "to exist." The lower character is the Japanese syllable *ri*, which indicates a noun form here.

WHAT IS YOI?

Often when you watch a karate tournament you will notice in the sparring segments that the competitors with the superior techniques are not always the ones who win the matches. A competitor who receives a minor injury during a match, for example, will suddenly become hesitant to attack, and, in spite of possessing superior skills, may lose even if the physical effects of the injury were negligible. Similarly, an exceptionally aggressive competitor can win more than his or her fair share of matches just relying on this trait alone.

This illustrates how matches can often be won or lost even before the competitors enter the ring. We are all aware of the importance of training hard and practicing our techniques before competition, but we sometimes forget a crucial aspect of our preparation: motivation, or the will to win.

The importance of motivation in preparing for any activity is illustrated by the Japanese word *yoi,* which means "ready." The first ideogram, *yo,* means "use" or "utilize," while the second, *i,* means "will" or "motivation." To be prepared is to be motivated.

There is a very well-known aspect of karate training in which the proper preparation of your will and motivation are crucial for success: breaking such items as boards and bricks with your bare hands. This is not very difficult, really; even a child can punch and split a board in two with just a bit of guidance. Success does, however, require firm belief that your chosen object is breakable. A shred of doubt will keep you from success, and can even cause serious injury, but if you firmly grasp an unshakeable belief that you can do it, you'll find the board or even brick is surprisingly fragile. A crucial part of preparation, then, is in your mind.

The ideogram *i* for motivation is made up of the radical *kokoro* for "heart" or "mind," and *on,* which in this case means "to force." This means that motivation is something we force into our mind. This is an image which can serve you well in karate. When you are facing competition in karate, for example, you should visualize this motivation swelling in your heart, and release it, along with all of your energy, at the outset of the match.

In karate, you will hear the word *yoi* before sparring, the performance of a **KATA,** and even simple calisthenics during warm up. This is the way in which the instructor or referee tells you to prepare yourself for the next task at hand. Each time you hear it, remember the true meaning of readiness in Japanese: to be prepared is to be motivated, or *yoi.*

Yo is a pictograph of a fence made out of wood, and developed the meaning of "function" or "utility."

I is a phonetic character. At the bottom is heart. The element at the top indicates pronunciation and means "to force." Together they mean to force something into the mind, or "consciousness," "motivation," or "will."

What is Kata?

*K*ata means "form." In karate the word refers to the method of practice by which students go through a series of techniques that have been arranged in a particular order. All Japanese martial arts, such as kendo and judo, have *kata* practice, but karate is the only one in which *kata* can be done by just one person.

You have probably seen a karate *kata* even if you did not know what the word meant until now. It is the exercise that can look like an intricate dance. Students throw punches, kicks and other techniques in the air, imagining opponents coming at them from all directions. Sometimes, it is very clear from their movements what they are doing. Other movements are more mysterious, and only experts who have studied karate for a long time know what they mean.

By repeating *kata* properly, over and over, your techniques will gradually improve, because proper form is the secret to striking with the most force and speed. *Kata* also develops balance, coordination, and mental discipline. It's not easy to practice a *kata* repeatedly with concentration, yet this is precisely what is required in proper *kata* training.

Another important aspect of *kata* is that it makes you a part of something bigger than yourself. Remember, your fellow classmates all study the same *kata*, and so did your instructor. If you attend a very traditional karate school, the *kata* you practice may be hundreds of years old, first developed by the great masters in ancient Okinawa or even China. And as you improve your karate to the point where you are teaching the *kata* to your own students, they will also will be carrying on this important tradition.

As you practice your *kata,* make sure each technique is as close to perfection as you can make it. Pay a great deal of attention to your stances, as techniques tend to appear very sloppy if you are not standing properly. Also, learn how to breathe properly and relax, as this will produce the best results.

Most important, however, is respecting your *kata*. You can do this by bowing properly before and after performing each one. By bowing you are recognizing the *kata's* tradition and history, and the efforts of all karate students who worked hard to learn it before you.

Kata is a combined-meaning phonetic character. The upper left element is a picture of a frame or pattern for construction. Next to it is a sword, which means "to make or to act." Together the upper elements came to mean to judge based on a frame or pattern (the law), and eventually "to punish."

The lower element of *kata* is a pictograph of earth, and was added to give this new character the meaning of "form" or "pattern."

What is Zanshin?

When you complete a **KATA**, it is customary to spend a few seconds looking at the direction of your last attack. Even as you return to a natural, standing position, you should maintain your focus in that same direction a few seconds longer. This makes sense when you consider *kata* to be a sequence of techniques against imaginary opponents. You have to make sure upon the completion of the *kata* that your last opponent has been completely dealt with, and will not be attacking you again. This is called *zanshin*.

The word is made up of two ideograms: *zan,* which means "to leave," and *shin,* which means "mind" or "consciousness." Therefore, *zanshin* is the act of setting aside a part of your conscious mind when you finish a *kata* in order to ensure that it is completed properly.

Of course, not properly maintaining your guard in a physical confrontation from start to finish can have dire consequences. Even an opponent who appears defeated may still be looking for opportunities for further attack.

He may even exploit a moment of distraction to pull out a weapon. *Zanshin* will get you in the habit of maintaining your guard until you are absolutely certain everything is safe.

As in most karate customs, however, the lesson to be gained from *zanshin* can be applied to other aspects of life. Many of us, in our eagerness to accomplish our tasks, rush through them and are inattentive to details and finishing touches. We may leave some dirt in the corners of the room while cleaning house, or rush through the annotations and make unnecessary errors when writing a term paper. Neglect of details can undermine all the efforts we have devoted to our work.

In both Asia and the West, something worth doing is worth doing well. Unfortunately, human nature is such that when we are eager to complete a task, we tend to become inattentive to detail. Karate provides the very useful practice of *zanshin* to help you get in the habit of not being distracted by the very goals you wish to attain.

Zan is a combined-meaning phonetic character. The left element is a picture of broken or smashed bones, and the right element is a picture of two halberds crossing in fierce battle, meaning "to hurt, harm, or cause loss." Together they express the meaning of extreme loss, to be left or leave behind.

 Shin is a pictograph depicting a heart. It expresses the meanings "heart," "mind," and "spirit."

What is Pinan (heian)?

Pinan in karate refers to a series of five **KATA** that are among the most widely practiced by beginners. *Pinan* is the original, Okinawan pronunciation, but because the first ideogram *pin* is pronounced *hei* in standard Japanese, some schools of karate call the kata *heian*. Whichever way it is pronounced, the first ideogram means "peace," while the second, *an*, means "tranquility." Together, the name symbolizes the ultimate goal of karate: to achieve tranquil peace both socially and spiritually.

The five *pinan kata* were developed by an Okinawan karate master, Yasutsune Itosu (1830–1915), who is recognized as one of the most influential figures in the history of karate. Because their movements exclude the more difficult techniques, the *kata* are taught to beginning and intermediate students of karate. Among the major schools of karate which include the *pinan (heian)* in their syllabus are Shito-Ryu, Shotokan, and Wado-Ryu.

The paradox that the ultimate goal of karate is non-violence is widely known but not always understood. On the one hand, there is no denying that some practitioners of karate only superficially recognize its peaceful aims, if at all, and simply learn its techniques so that they can win their fights in bars and on the street.

Meanwhile, people who have heard only about the philosophical, spiritual aspects of karate are often shocked to see the fierce aggression displayed by students when they visit an actual school. They expect old karate masters with long white beards who talk of love and harmony to students who gently go through their drills in a dreamy fashion. They do not understand that karate, ultimately, is the art of fighting, and one cannot fight well without aggression.

Both approaches to karate are misguided. To practice karate is to recognize that the ultimate goal of our society is to evolve into one in which all its members can live peacefully and fruitfully. At the same time, it is also necessary to recognize the inescapable fact that our society still gives rise to violent situations, and that in order to deal with them, violent reactions are sometimes necessary.

In order to determine whether violence is necessary, we must be able to see the situation objectively. Yet we must always be extremely prudent, for any act of violence, no matter how well-justified it may seem, can have terrible consequences. This tension between the ideal and the real is a point of much self-reflection for the true student of karate. Through reflection and meditation, the student moves closer to the second objective of karate, expressed in the name of the *pinan kata:* peace and tranquility of the spirit through a greater understanding of one's self.

That Itosu gave a name with such profound meaning to a handful of basic *kata* seems to indicate the importance he placed on teaching these truths to students from the beginning.

Pin is pronounced *hei* in standard Japanese. It is a pictograph depicting water plants floating evenly on the water surface, and it expresses the meanings "level," "flat," and "even."

An is a pictograph. The lower element is a woman sitting. Above her is a picture of a roof. Together they express the meaning of peace and contentment.

What is Sanchin?

Sanchin is a **Kata** that builds muscular strength, improves blood circulation, and helps develop proper breathing methods.

Sanchin has existed since ancient times in Fujien Province in southern China, but was altered and further developed by the Okinawan karate master Kanryo Higaonna (1852–1915). Schools of karate that practice *sanchin* include Shito-Ryu and Goju-Ryu. A somewhat different version of *sanchin,* independent of Higaonna's alterations, is also practiced by students of Uechi-Ryu.

The *san* in *sanchin* means three, while the second ideogram, *chin,* is written as "battle" or "conflict." (Although the second ideogram is pronounced *sen* in standard Japanese, the *kata* has retained its Okinawan name.) *Sanchin* is the *kata* of three challenges.

What are they?

We can interpret the three challenges at several levels. On the most practical level they are the challenges of properly developing our muscles, blood circulation, and breathing. *Sanchin* is also recognized as the *kata* that develops the metaphysical energy called *ki* (see **Kiai** and **Tanden**). The paths that *ki* travels through the body are said to converge at three points: the top of the head, the lower abdomen, and the feet.

On another level, *sanchin* can be interpreted as three aspects of the lives of all of us: the past, present, and future. Unless we take up the challenge of studying all three time periods, our understanding of our lives will be incomplete.

The three aims of *sanchin* can also be interpreted as the development the body, the mind, and the techniques of karate. If you are endowed with a strong body and proficient techniques but not a sound mind, there is a danger you will misuse karate. If you have a sound mind with healthy morals but not the strength and fighting techniques to defend them, you will be impotent. Even lacking just a single element, whether technique or physical strength, will result in an unbalanced understanding of karate, because technique relies on physical ability, while physical ability by itself cannot be taught to others.

Finally, in life we can be in conflict with other people, our surroundings, or our inner selves. To live harmoniously with all three aspects of our lives, to successfully meet all the challenges of *sanchin* on every level, is the ultimate goal of karate study.

San is a diagrammatic character. The three strokes represent the number three.

Chin, pronounced *sen* in standard Japanese, is a phonetic character. The element on the right is a halberd, the most deadly weapon in ancient China. The element on the left indicates pronunciation, and also means "to fight." Together they mean "fight," "battle," or "challenge."

What is Budo?

The Japanese refer to their modern martial arts as *budo,* which means "the martial way" or "the way of a warrior." The more classical arts are usually called *bujutsu,* which means "martial techniques." *Bujutsu* include *jujutsu,* out of which developed the more modern judo; *kenjutsu,* out of which came kendo; and *aikijutsu,* out of which developed aikido, judo, kendo, and aikido are *budo,* as is karate.

The difference between *bujutsu* and *budo* is usually a matter of emphasis. The classical arts generally are associated more closely with war, and therefore place greater emphasis on self-defense techniques that are too dangerous for use in friendly competition. Although experts of modern *budo* are also skilled in these techniques, they stress such matters as safety and martial arts as something everyone, young and old, can practice with enjoyment. With the exception of *aikido,* the modern arts include the practice of free sparring and encourage competitive tournaments, which would be impossible to conduct with lethal techniques.

Another difference in emphasis can be seen in the use of the word *do* in *budo. Do* means "the way," the path the human spirit travels through life, from birth to death. Although spiritual reflection was also a part of classical martial arts training, greater emphasis has been placed upon it by the modern arts.

There are other traditional Japanese arts which also define themselves through the concept of *do,* such as *sado,* the tea ceremony or "the way of tea," and *shodo,* calligraphy, or "the way of writing." While all reflect meditatively on our spiritual journey through life, *budo* distinguishes itself by its awareness of the journey's perils.

The first ideogram *bu* is made up of the radicals *hoko,* which refers to the halberd, a spear-like weapon, underneath which is a derivative of *matagu,* or "to stride," combining to create the image of stepping forth with a weapon. Martial artists should be aware that they stride down their spiritual paths with weapon in hand, and above all they should appreciate the possibility that their journey can, in some unfortunate circumstances, end suddenly and abruptly. This should serve to make them realize the value of their own lives and those of others.

As the great karate master Gichin Funakoshi (1869–1957) once said, "There is no first strike in karate." Quite often, violence only winds up causing more violence, and can result in catastrophe. The proper way to use your skills in karate is with great caution and much appreciation of life's fragility.

While karate's origins lie in ancient Okinawa and China, its spread through Japan and the rest of the world is a modern phenomenon, as are many of its methods of training and its emphasis on spirituality. This places it among other Japanese *budo.*

Bu is a phonetic character. The element on top is a halberd and also indicates the pronunciation. The element below is a foot, meaning to advance. Together they originally expressed the meaning of one step forward. Eventually they came to mean military strength or power.

Do is a phonetic character. The left side shows a foot, below, walking down lines representing a road. Together they express the meanings "road" or "way." The element to the right indicates the character's pronunciation.

What is Zen?

Zen is a form of Buddhism that originated in China in the sixth century and has gone through much development and change in Japan since it arrived there during the twelfth century. Its teachings affected many traditional Japanese art forms, among them flower arranging, painting, calligraphy, and the martial arts, including, of course, karate.

Zen stresses the importance of living our daily lives to the fullest. To do this, we must be able to see the world around us in its true form at each moment in time. Our perceptions, however, are influenced by our own biases. Only by understanding ourselves can we understand our biases, and thereby truly observe reality. Zen also practices self-reflection through meditation. Knowing just this much about Zen, you can recognize its influence on karate, in the practice of **Mokuso,** for instance.

According to Zen, enlightenment is the attainment of emptiness or nothingness. This nothingness, however, does not mean that you no longer exist. Rather, it is like a mirror, which reflects everything, and leaves nothing of itself, even though it is still there. If you can see reality as it is without bias, just as a mirror reflects its surroundings, you have achieved enlightenment.

Recognizing your own biases, however, is by no means easy. For example, there was once a karate student who was extremely skilled. One day a common street thug insulted him, and the student fought back and beat the thug badly.

But when his teacher learned of the incident, he scolded the student for using karate without discretion. In his defense, the student said he did not provoke the fight. The thug had insulted him and he was only defending his honor. "I see," said the teacher. "Then if I insulted you in the same way, you would fight me as well?"

The student quickly replied, "Oh, no, Sensei. Your skills in karate are far superior to my own. I would never be able to defeat you."

The teacher shook his head. "Then it would seem," he said, "you fought this poor man only because you knew you could defeat him."

When the student realized he had deluded himself into believing he had fought for his honor when in truth he used his skills in karate out of conceit and pride, he bowed and humbly asked for his teacher's forgiveness. Because karate can be a destructive force when not used properly, it is very important to constantly reflect on yourself and your actions as you continue your studies.

禅 *Zen* is a phonetic character. The element on the left is a picture of the wooden platform which was prepared for the descent of the gods to receive their sacrifices. The right side indicates pronunciation and also means a flat area of ground prepared by the emperor for festivals dedicated to the gods.

In Chinese it is pronounced *chan*, and it was used to transliterate the Sanskrit word *dhyana*, or "meditation"—the main practice of Zen Buddhism.

What is Osu?

People who study karate can often be heard saying the word *osu*. Sometimes they will say it in a normal speaking voice, but just as often, they will loudly shout this word, which can substitute for "hello," "good-bye," "yes," "okay," or "I understand." No matter how or when it is said, however, *osu* reaffirms one of the most important lessons of karate.

The top character, *o*, means to push, and symbolizes one hundred percent effort. The second character, *su*, means to endure. Combined, *osu* is a pledge to do one's very best and to endure. However, *su* by itself can also mean "to be silent," and the character is made up of the radicals meaning "blade" and "heart." The Japanese idea of endurance, therefore, encompasses being silent, even if your heart is cut with a blade.

It is very natural for people to seek positive reinforcement in return for their efforts. This is the very principle by which our society operates, after all. Professionals are paid for their work. Teachers reward hard-working students with high marks. Parents pay children compliments for their efforts.

But karate is a discipline which involves a great deal of self-reflection, and self-reflection is more concerned with irrefutable truths than with rewards. Unfortunately, there are some karate students who pretend to work hard only when they believe their instructor is watching. These types of students devote more energy toward attracting their teacher's attention than to learning karate. In other words, their efforts are not "silent."

What these students do not realize is that they are in class to learn karate, not to impress the teacher. And how much they learn depends solely on how hard they work. If they give their best efforts only when the instructor is watching and are lazy the rest of the time, this will inevitably be reflected in their technique.

On the other hand, true karate masters are usually humble and reserved. They realize their expertise in karate and the amount of effort they have devoted to it are irrefutable, independent of the recognition of others. After all, a flower blossoming deep in a secluded forest is no less beautiful than one growing in a garden where everyone can see. In fact, many great karate masters have spent time training on secluded mountains in Japan, where they had to continually challenge themselves to work hard even though there was no one there to provide encouragement or reinforcement.

Each time you say *osu* during karate class, remember that it is a pledge to work hard and to endure. If you can say it honestly and with pride each time, you can be confident you are doing well.

O is a phonetic character. The left element is a hand, and the right element indicates pronunciation and also means "to push," "to control," "to suppress," which is the meaning of both elements together as well.

Su is a phonetic character. The lower element is a picture of a heart, and the upper element indicates pronunciation and also means "to endure." Together they mean "to bear," "to endure," or "to conceal."

What is Rei?

They say karate begins and ends with *rei,* which means "respect," as well as "courtesy." As mentioned elsewhere in this book, karate students treat not only people with respect, but also such things as their school and uniforms. What this means is that we do not take these things for granted. The left radical in *rei* means "deity" while the right signifies "bounty." In other words, *rei* is the spirit of giving thanks for bounty. It is the appreciation of good fortune.

What would karate practice be like without *rei*? Certainly, students would not learn as much, for listening attentively to the instructor and not talking out of turn is an important part of *rei*. It would also be more dangerous, because cooperating to ensure a karate class is safe is also a part of *rei*. Without it, people would be free to disrupt class or cause unnecessary injury. In karate, as in society, smooth interaction relies greatly on courtesy and respecting social conventions.

The way in which karate students express their respect most is by bowing. Students bow to the teacher before and after class. They also bow to each other before starting to work together in drills or sparring. Even before and after competition matches, which contestants try their hardest to win, they bow to express their mutual respect. After all, it takes courage and determination to enter and train for competition.

By showing *rei* during karate class, students and teachers are saying they appreciate the opportunity to learn from each other. And by treating their classmates with courtesy and respect, students also recognize the hard work and discipline that everyone is devoting to karate. By treating things such as their school and uniforms with respect, they make certain they do not take these things for granted. Remember, not everyone is fortunate enough to be able to learn karate.

Apply the principles of *rei* to life outside of karate class, and you have simple etiquette. Thanking guests for coming to your party is an indication that you appreciate the effort they made to attend. Proper table manners are an expression of your respect for your dining partners' right to enjoy a pleasant meal without being offended.

As you become accustomed to expressing *rei* in karate class, see if you can show similar attention to the etiquette of daily living. And never take good people, nor good things, for granted. That is the spirit of *rei*.

Rei is a phonetic character. The element on the left is a picture of the wooden platform which was prepared for the descent of the gods to receive their sacrifices. The element on the right indicates pronunciation and also means "to carry out."

Together they express the meaning of the proper ceremony to be carried out when worshiping the gods and, by extension, the rules of behavior that all people should observe.

GLOSSARY

of Other Commonly Used Words in Karate

Counting from 1 to 10:

Ichi 1

Ni 2

San 3

Shi (Yon) 4

Go 5

Roku 6

Shichi (Nana) 7

Hachi 8

Kyu (Ku) 9

Jyu 10

Hajime Begin

Yame Stop

Mae Front

Ushiro Back

Jodan Upper

Chudan Middle

Gedan Lower

Oizuki Straight Punch

Gyakuzuki Reverse Punch

Kagizuki Hook

Kizamizuki Jab

Zuzuki Head Butt

Uraken Backfist

Empi (Hiji) Elbow

Uchi Strike

Shuto Knife Hand

Maegeri Front Kick

Yokogeri Side Kick

Mawashigeri Roundhouse Kick

Ushirogeri Back Kick

Hizageri Knee Kick

Uke Block

Harai (Barai) Parry

Sabaki Turning the body to avoid a strike

The "weathermark" identifies this book as a production of Weatherhill, Inc., publishers of fine books on Asia and the Pacific. Editorial supervision: Jeffrey Hunter. Book design and typography: Mariana Canelo. Cover design: David S. Noble. Production supervision: Bill Rose. Printed and bound at Daamen, Inc., West Rutland, Vermont. The typeface used is Scala.